D0845995

THE TERRA-COTTA ARMY

DIGGING UP THE PAST

BY EMILY ROSE OACHS

TORQUE™

TM

Are you ready to take it to the xtreme? Torque books thrust you nto the action-packed world of ports, vehicles, mystery, and dventure. These books may include irt, smoke, fire, and chilling tales. VARNING: read at your own risk.

his edition first published in 2020 by Bellwether Media, Inc.

brary of Congress Cataloging-in-Publication Data

lames: Oachs, Emily Rose, author.
itle: The Terra-Cotta Army / by Emily Rose Oachs.
escription: Minneapolis, MN : Bellwether Media, Inc., 2020. | Series: Torque: Digging Up the Past | Includes bibliographical references and index. | Audience: Grades 3-7. | Audience: Ages 7-12.
dentifiers: LCCN 2018061018 (print) | LCCN 2019001752 (ebook) | ISBN 9781618916426 (ebook) | ISBN 9781644870709 (hardcover : alk. paper)
ubjects: LCSH: Qin shi huang, Emperor of China, 259-210 B.C.–Tomb–Juvenile literature. | Terra-cotta sculpture, Chinese–Qin-Han dynasties, 221 B.C.-220 A.D.–Juvenile literature. | Shaanxi Sheng (China)–Antiquities–Juvenile literature.
lassification: LCC DS747.9.C47 (ebook) | LCC DS747.9.C47 O23 2020 (print) | DDC 931/.04–dc23
C record available at https://lccn.loc.gov/2018061018

Editor: Betsy Rathburn Designer: Brittany McIntosh

Printed in the United States of America, North Mankato, MN.

TABLE OF CONTENTS

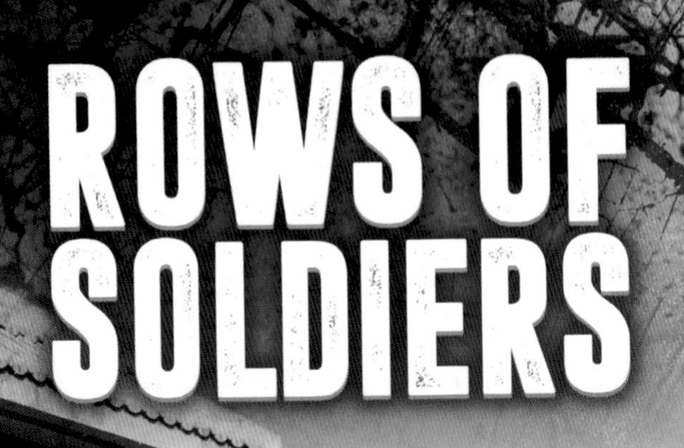

ROWS OF SOLDIERS

You walk towards a group of large buildings. What wonders do they hold? You climb the steps to the nearest building. Inside, you find a huge, open space.

Rows of clay soldiers stretch out before you. Clay horses stand among them. All have been dug up from the earth. You are looking at the ruler Qin Shihuang's **terra-cotta** army!

QIN SHIHUANG

Qin Shihuang is pronounced CHIN shuhr-HWANG.

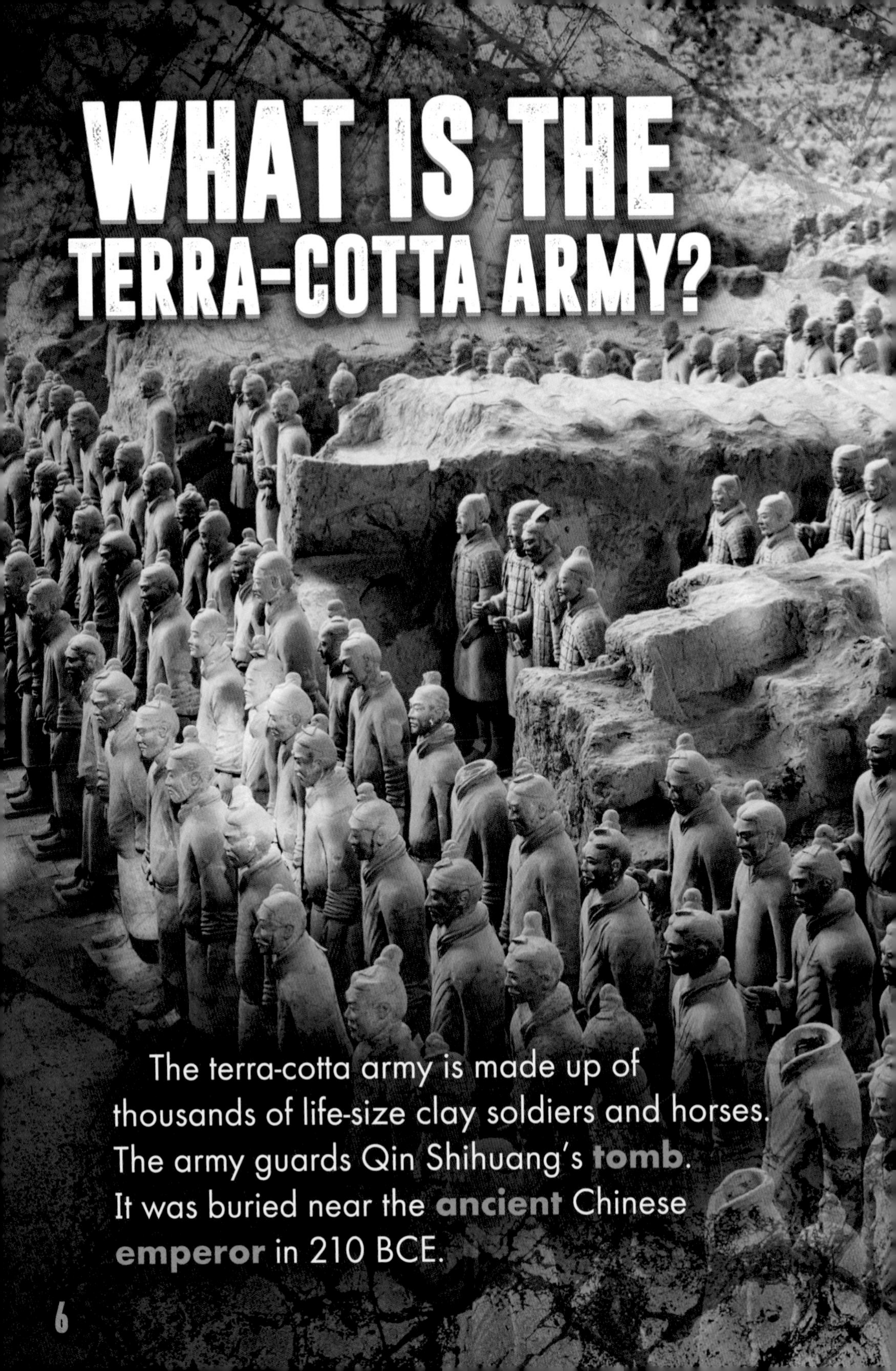

WHAT IS THE TERRA-COTTA ARMY?

The terra-cotta army is made up of thousands of life-size clay soldiers and horses. The army guards Qin Shihuang's **tomb**. It was buried near the **ancient** Chinese **emperor** in 210 BCE.

The emperor's large burial **complex** stands near Xi'an, China. It is at the foot of Lishan Mountain. It is the largest tomb ever found in China!

WHERE IS THE TERRA-COTTA ARMY?

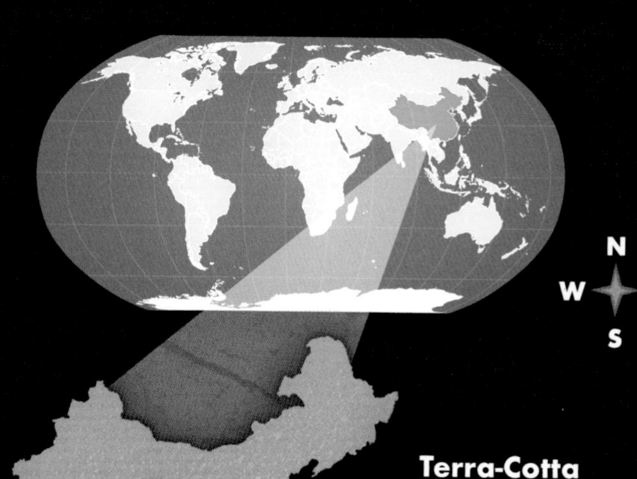

Qin Shihuang was born as Ying Zheng. In 246 BCE, he began ruling the powerful Chinese state of Qin. Construction of his burial site began soon after.

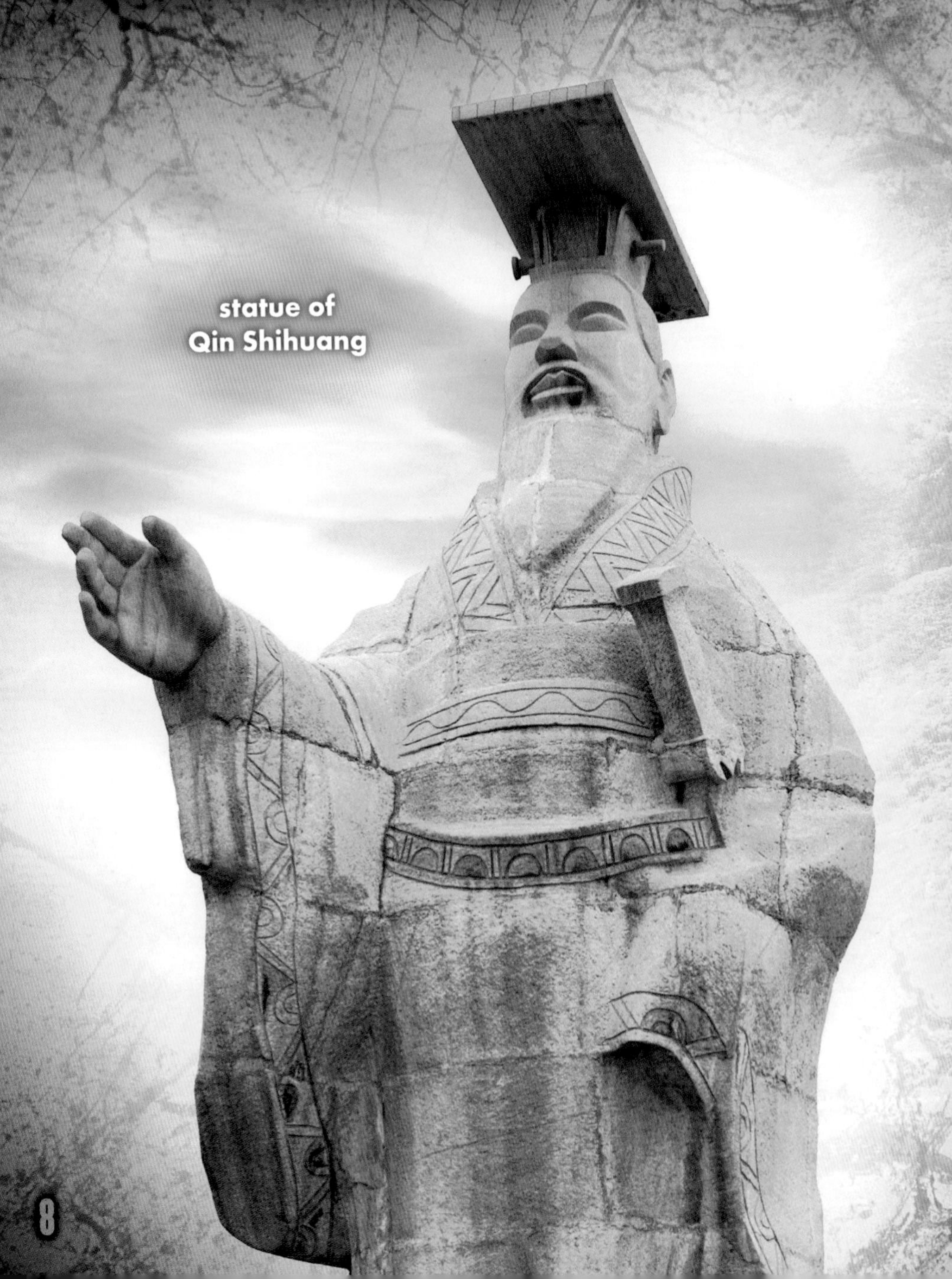

statue of Qin Shihuang

BIG CHANGES

Qin Shihuang's rule brought many changes. People across China began using the same measurements and laws. Workers built roads to connect all of China. Construction on the Great Wall began.

Great Wall of China

Qin Shihuang took control of the six other Chinese states. In 221 BCE, he was the first emperor to **unify** China. His time in power later became known as the Qin **dynasty**.

Experts are not certain why Qin Shihuang had the army built. Many think it was meant to protect him in the **afterlife**.

Soon after Qin Shihuang's death, his enemies broke into the burial site. They stole weapons. They shattered many terra-cotta figures. They set a fire that ruined much of the underground space. The emperor's burial site and clay army were forgotten.

TERRA-COTTA ARMY TIMELINE

246 BCE:
Ying Zheng becomes leader of the Chinese state of Qin at age 13

221 BCE:
Emperor Qin Shihuang unifies all of China under his

210 BCE:
Qin Shihuang dies

206 BCE:
The Qin dynasty ends and the Han dynasty begins

BUILDING FOR THE BURIAL

The burial site took nearly 40 years to complete! Construction did not end until about two years after Qin Shihuang died.

1974 CE:
Farmers digging a well discover pieces from the clay army buried near Qin Shihuang

1979:
The Museum of the Terra-Cotta Army opens

1987:
Qin Shihuang's burial complex becomes a UNESCO World Heritage Site

FOUND AT LAST

In March 1974 CE, some farmers were digging a well. As they dug, they found pieces of clay figures. The discovery led to a large **excavation**.

Archaeologists unearthed one clay soldier after another. Most were in pieces. Experts worked to **restore** the figures. They carefully pieced the figures back together.

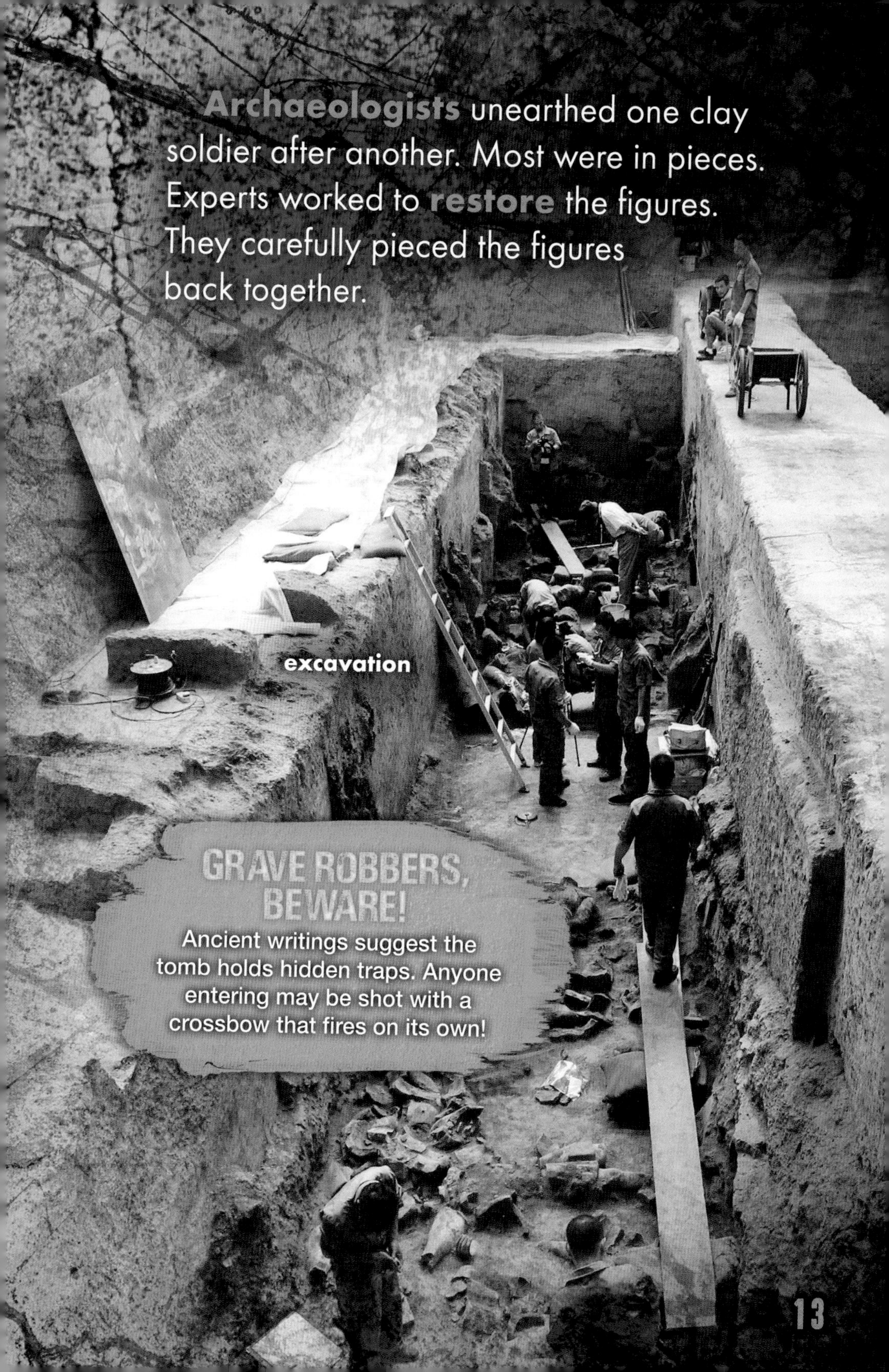

excavation

GRAVE ROBBERS, BEWARE!

Ancient writings suggest the tomb holds hidden traps. Anyone entering may be shot with a crossbow that fires on its own!

Archaeologists are still studying the soldiers. They believe there are at least 8,000! The soldiers are arranged for battle. They once held weapons such as swords and crossbows. Clay horses and wooden **chariots** were buried nearby.

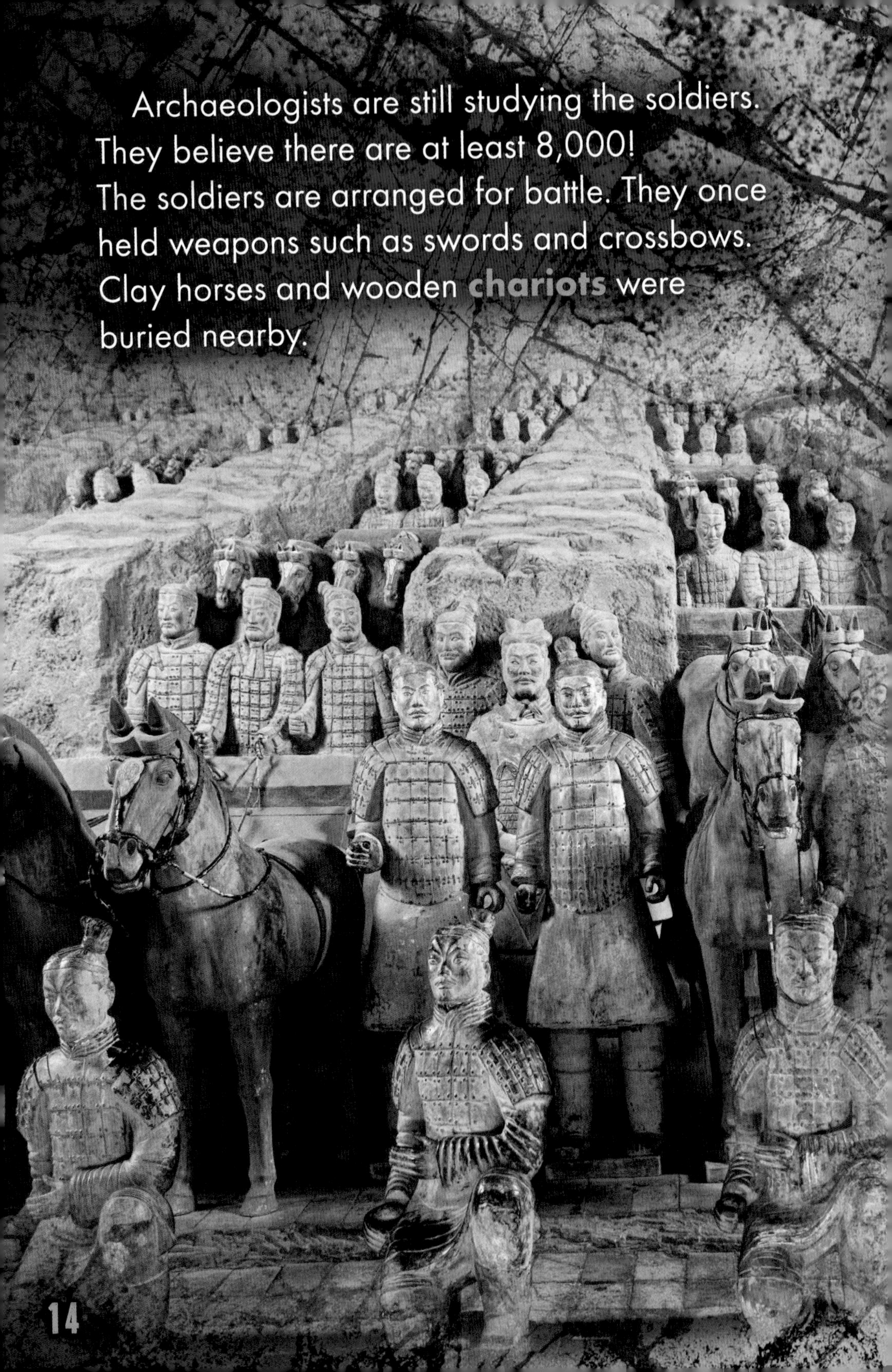

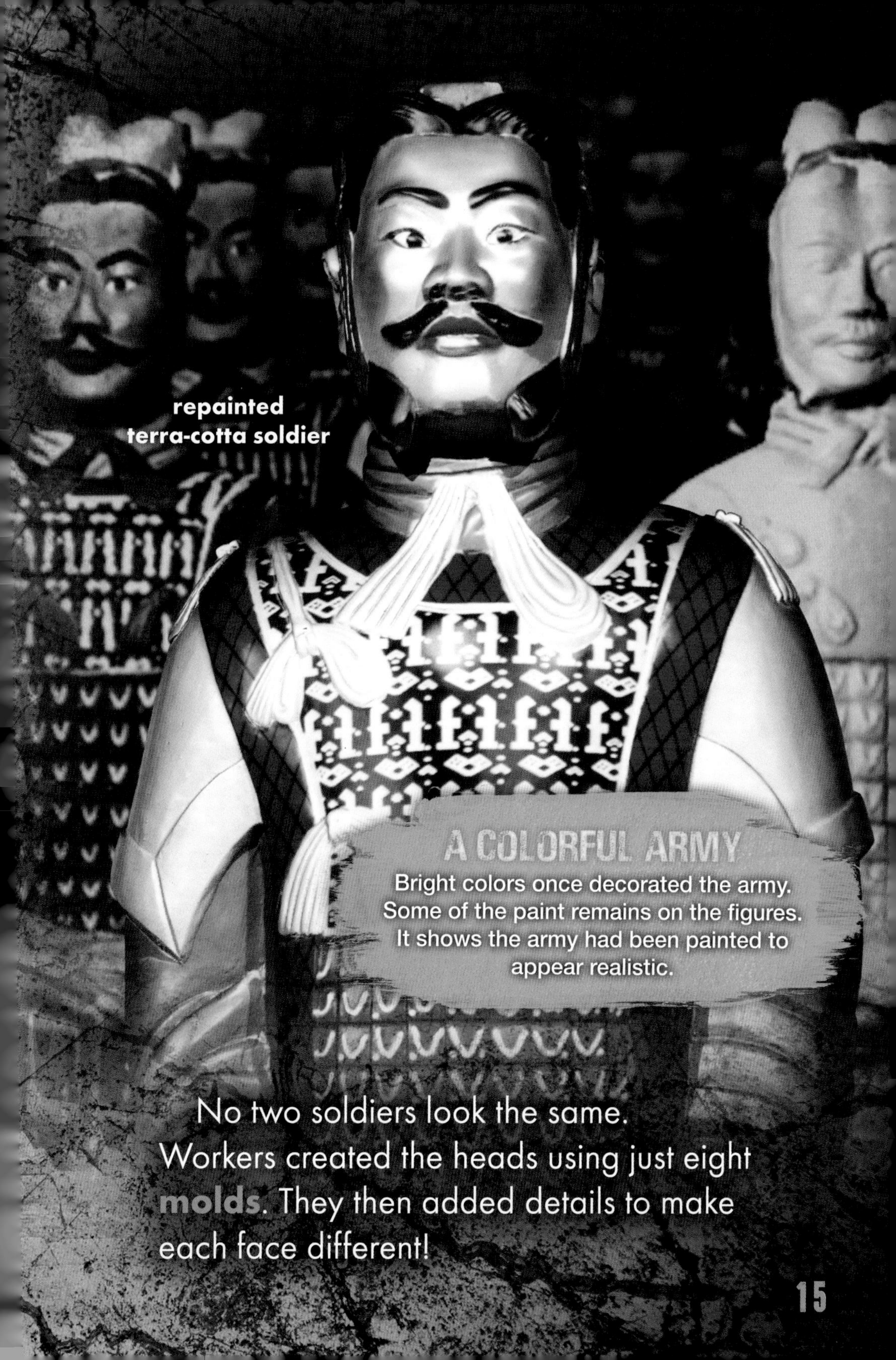

A COLORFUL ARMY

Bright colors once decorated the army. Some of the paint remains on the figures. It shows the army had been painted to appear realistic.

No two soldiers look the same. Workers created the heads using just eight **molds**. They then added details to make each face different!

Experts discovered the soldiers in three main underground pits. These make up a small part of the emperor's burial site. The entire site covers nearly 38 square miles (98 square kilometers)!

Nearby pits hold bones from horses and other animals. There are also tombs where workers were buried.

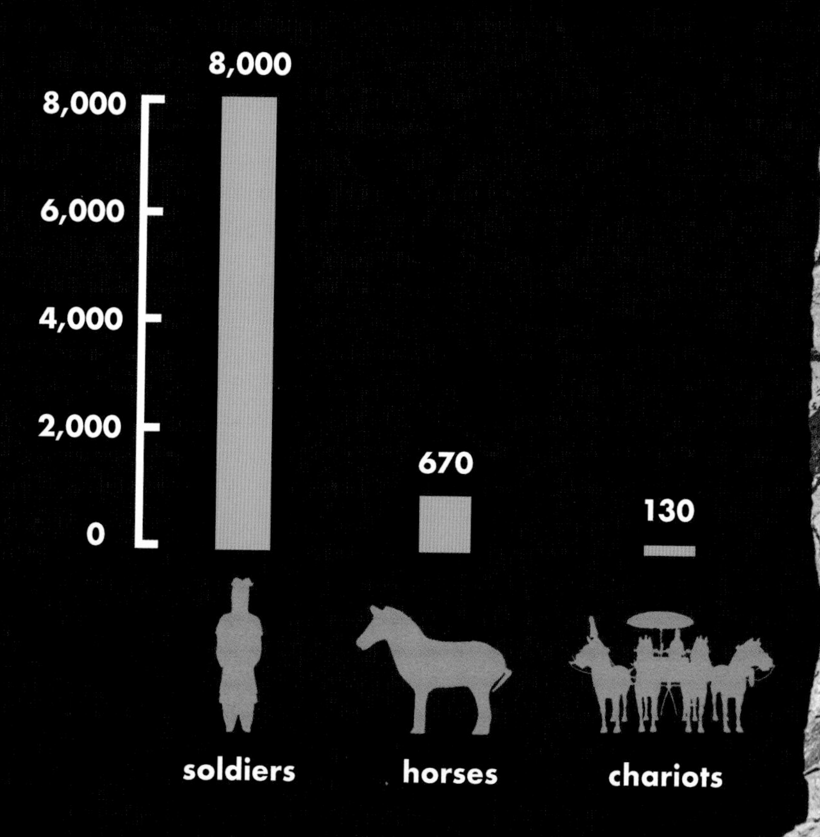

FIGHTING TO PRESERVE

Little of the burial site has been excavated. Many soldiers likely remain buried. Qin Shihuang's tomb also sits untouched.

Archaeologists are slow to uncover more. They worry about their **preservation** methods. Their methods may not be advanced enough to keep the **artifacts** safe. They want to be able to unearth new artifacts without causing harm.

PRESERVING THE PAST IN PAINT

Discovery: Paint on the terra-cotta army can be preserved using new methods
Date of Discovery: 1994
Process:

1. New methods were needed to keep paint on newly excavated soldiers from fading or flaking
2. Tried many chemicals to preserve the paint before settling on polyethylene glycol (PEG)
3. Wrapped soldiers in plastic to keep from drying out

What It Means:

- Easier to see army as it originally looked
- Army will be easier to preserve for long periods of time
- Future discoveries more easily preserved

The Museum of the Terra-Cotta Army opened in 1979. It was built over the long pits where the army was discovered.

tourists

Millions of **tourists** visit each year. They see the restored army stand as it was found. Two thousand years after Qin Shihuang's death, the terra-cotta army still guards his grave!

GLOSSARY

afterlife—the place some people believe exists after death

ancient—very old

archaeologists—scientists who study the remains of past human life and activities

artifacts—objects that save the history and culture of a past event or place

chariots—vehicles pulled by horses

complex—a structure that is made up of many parts

dynasty—a line of rulers that come from the same family; ancient Chinese history is divided into dynasties.

emperor—a ruler

excavation—the act of digging up

molds—containers that give clay or other materials shape; material hardens in molds and holds its shape when removed.

preservation—protection

restore—to rebuild an object to look as it once did

terra-cotta—a type of clay that can be baked to make pottery or statues

tomb—a building where a person is placed after death

tourists—people who travel to visit another place

unify—to bring many pieces together as one

TO LEARN MORE

AT THE LIBRARY

Capek, Michael. *Secrets of the Terracotta Army*. North Mankato, Minn.: Capstone Press, 2015.

Compestine, Ying Chang. *Secrets of the Terra-Cotta Soldier*. New York, N.Y.: Amulet Books, 2014.

Kenney, Karen Latchana. *Mysteries of the Great Wall of China*. Minneapolis, Minn.: Lerner Publications, 2018.

ON THE WEB

FACTSURFER

Factsurfer.com gives you a safe, fun way to find more information.

1. Go to www.factsurfer.com.
2. Enter "terra-cotta army" into the search box and click 🔍.
3. Select your book cover to see a list of related web sites.

INDEX

The images in this book are reproduced through the courtesy of: Efired, front cover; John Goulter/ Alamy, p. 4; Jarno Gonzalez Zarraonandia, p. 5; Oleksiy Maksymenko Photography/ Alamy, pp. 6-7; Henry Westheim Photography/ Alamy, p. 8; Hung Chung Chih, p. 9; Phraisohn Siripool, pp. 10-11; imageBROKER/ Alamy, p. 12; STR/ Stringer/ Getty Images, p. 13; DnDavis, p. 14; Hemis/ Alamy, p. 15; George Oze/ Alamy, p. 16; Rosemarie Stennull/ Alamy, pp. 18-19; VCG/ Contributor/ Getty Images, pp. 20-21.